T0402945

SPIDERS: EIGHT-LEGGED TERRORS

GIANT HUNTSMAN SPIDERS

BY MELISSA RAÉ SHOFNER

Gareth Stevens
PUBLISHING

Please visit our website, www.garethstevens.com. For a free color catalog of all our high-quality books, call toll free 1-800-542-2595 or fax 1-877-542-2596.

Cataloging-in-Publication Data

Names: Shofner, Melissa Raé.
Title: Giant huntsman spiders / Melissa Raé Shofner.
Description: New York : Gareth Stevens Publishing, 2018. | Series: Spiders: eight-legged terrors | Includes index.
Identifiers: ISBN 9781538202098 (pbk.) | ISBN 9781538202111 (library bound) | ISBN 9781538202104 (6 pack)
Subjects: LCSH: Spiders–Juvenile literature.
Classification: LCC QL458.4 S56 2018 | DDC 595.4'4–dc23

First Edition

Published in 2018 by
Gareth Stevens Publishing
111 East 14th Street, Suite 349
New York, NY 10003

Designer: Laura Bowen
Editor: Ryan Nagelhout

Photo credits: Cover, p. 1 (spider) Josve05a/Wikimedia Commons; cover, pp. 1–24 (background) Fantom666/Shutterstock.com; cover, pp. 1–24 (black splatter) Miloje/Shutterstock.com; cover, pp. 1–24 (web) Ramona Kaulitzki/Shutterstock.com; pp. 4–24 (text boxes) Tueris/Shutterstock.com; pp. 5 (main), 17 kurt_G/Shutterstock.com; p. 5 (inset) Ethically Yours/Wikimedia Commons; p. 7 (world map) Sarefo/Wikimedia Commons; p. 7 (Laos map) Hdamm/Wikimedia Commons; p. 9 (top) Stuart Wilson/Getty Images; p. 9 (bottom) niyoseris/Shutterstock.com; p. 11 Thomas Marent/Minden Pictures/Getty Images; p. 13 (top) Peter Waters/Shutterstock.com; p. 13 (bottom) Robert Pickett/Getty Images; p. 15 Ch'ien Lee/Minden Pictures/Getty Images; p. 19 Brian Cooper/Getty Images; p. 21 John Serrao/Getty Images.

Printed in China

CPSIA compliance information: Batch #CS17GS: For further information contact Gareth Stevens, New York, New York at 1-800-542-2595.

CONTENTS

A Big Discovery 4

World Travelers 6

Long Legs! 8

Spiders in Hiding 10

On the Hunt 12

Spider Mom 14

Social Spiders 16

Huntsman Spiders and Humans 18

Spiders in Danger? 20

Glossary 22

For More Information 23

Index 24

Words in the glossary appear in **bold** type the first time they are used in the text.

A BIG DISCOVERY

Huntsman spiders are big, and they move really fast! They got their name because they hunt down their **prey** rather than catching it in a web. They may look scary, but they're harmless to humans. In fact, many people find huntsman spiders helpful when it comes to pest control.

In 2001, a German scientist discovered a new species, or kind, of huntsman spider. It was much bigger than other huntsman spiders. Due to its size, the new species was called the giant huntsman.

TERRIFYING TRUTHS

Huntsman spiders usually live for about 2 years, but they may live longer.

Giant huntsman are much bigger—and harrier—than the many other huntsman spiders.

5

WORLD TRAVELERS

Most species of huntsman spiders are native to Asia, but they can be found around the world in places with warm **climates**. Many kinds of huntsman spiders live in Australia. They're found in Southeast Asia, Europe, South Africa, South America, and New Zealand, too.

Huntsman spiders also live in Hawaii and in states across the southern United States, including Florida, Texas, Alabama, and California. The giant huntsman spider, however, has only been found in Laos, a Southeast Asian country bordering Thailand.

TERRIFYING TRUTHS

Huntsman spiders may have spread around the world by hiding in boxes of bananas that were shipped out of Asia!

HUNTSMAN SPIDER RANGE

North America

Europe

Asia

Africa

South America

Indian Ocean

Pacific Ocean

Atlantic Ocean

Australia

Laos

huntsman spider range

giant huntsman spider range

Huntsman spiders have been found in more than 25 countries around the world.

7

LONG LEGS!

The giant huntsman is the biggest spider in the world if you're judging by **leg span**. Its leg span can reach 12 inches (30 cm), which is about the size of a dinner plate! Other species of huntsman spider have an average leg span of about 5 to 6 inches (13 to 15 cm).

Huntsman spiders are also called giant crab spiders. This is because their legs bend like crab legs. This allows them to run fast and move from side to side. It also helps them climb straight up smooth surfaces such as glass!

TERRIFYING TRUTHS

The goliath bird-eating tarantula is also really big! It's the largest spider in the world based on body mass.

crab

If a spider's legs bend out to the sides and forward, rather than upward and under the body, it's probably a huntsman spider.

9

SPIDERS IN HIDING

Huntsman spiders are big, but they're good at staying out of sight. Many species are brown or gray, which helps them blend in with their **environment**. Their legs may be banded, or striped. Some huntsman spiders even have flat bodies that allow them to hide under loose tree bark, between rocks, and in small cracks in walls.

Giant huntsman spiders look like other huntsman species, but they're lighter in color. Scientists believe they live deep inside caves in Laos.

TERRIFYING TRUTHS

In Australia, huntsman spiders are often found hiding inside people's homes and cars! They're very shy!

Huntsman spiders can be hard to see even though they're quite large.

ON THE HUNT

Unlike many other spiders, huntsman spiders don't use webs to catch their food. Instead, they hunt their prey. This hunting action is how they got their name. Huntsman spiders are carnivores, which means they eat meat. Their favorite meals include bugs, frogs, lizards, and even other spiders.

Huntsman spiders use their speed and **agility** to chase their prey. When they get close enough, they strike! Huntsman spiders use their sharp **fangs** to kill their prey with **venom** before chowing down.

TERRIFYING TRUTHS

Huntsman spiders will hunt many kinds of small animals. Sometimes they'll even eat mice!

fangs

Huntsman spiders need to be quick to catch their prey. Their long legs help them move at speeds of up to 3 feet (0.9 m) per second!

13

SPIDER MOM

Huntsman spiders don't spin webs, but they do produce silk. A mother huntsman will make a silk sac and lay up to 200 eggs inside. She'll hide the sac under a piece of bark or a rock. Some species carry their egg sacs while they move around.

It takes about 3 weeks for the eggs to **hatch**. During this time, a mother huntsman will guard her egg sac if she doesn't carry it. She won't even leave to eat! She'll continue to protect her babies, called spiderlings, once they hatch.

TERRIFYING TRUTHS

As a baby huntsman grows, its skin becomes too small and peels off. This is called molting. The old skin often looks just like a real spider!

A mother huntsman spider can be very **aggressive**. She'll stay with her babies for several weeks to keep them safe.

15

SOCIAL SPIDERS

Most spiders live alone and don't usually spend time with other spiders. However, members of *Delena cancerides*, a species of huntsman spider, live in large groups called colonies. These spiders are sometimes called social huntsman spiders.

Social huntsman spiders are native to Australia. They build their colonies under the bark of dead trees. Several hundred spiders may live and work together. The mother spider keeps the colony safe while the other spiders go off to hunt.

TERRIFYING TRUTHS

There are more than 43,000 species of spiders on Earth, but only 60 are known to live in groups. Scientists are trying to understand why *Delena cancerides* live together in colonies.

Since spiders sometimes eat their own kind, living together could be unsafe for smaller species!

HUNTSMAN SPIDERS AND HUMANS

Giant huntsman spiders live in Laos far away from your home, but other huntsman spiders sometimes end up inside people's homes and cars. Luckily, most aren't usually aggressive. They may bite if they're bothered too much, but don't worry—it only hurts a little.

Some people may feel sick, throw up, or get a headache after being bitten by a huntsman. However, pain and swelling are often the only side effects. An ice pack should help, but see a doctor if the bite continues to hurt.

TERRIFYING TRUTHS

Huntsman spiders are great at catching bothersome bugs such as cockroaches. Some people like having these big spiders around for pest control!

Would you be afraid if a huge spider crawled up your arm?

SPIDERS IN DANGER?

What happens when the hunter becomes the hunted? Huntsman spiders make tasty snacks for birds, spider wasps, **parasitic** worms, and lizards such as geckos. The young of certain wasps and flies live inside a huntsman's eggs as parasites.

If you see a huntsman spider, try to stay calm. Remember that these large spiders don't want to hurt you. These spiders are speedy, but an adult may be able to help you carefully catch a huntsman and move it to a safe place outside.

TERRIFYING TRUTHS

Giant huntsman spiders are **rare** and only live in Laos, so it's unlikely you'll ever see one in real life. Other huntsman species are much more common.

Huntsman spiders may look scary, but they play an important part in keeping the number of pests down.

GLOSSARY

aggressive: ready to fight

agility: the ability to move around quickly and easily

climate: the average weather conditions of a place over a period of time

environment: all the living things and conditions of a place

fang: a hard, sharp-pointed body part a spider uses to put venom into its prey

hatch: to break open and let the young out

leg span: the distance from the tip of one leg to the tip of the leg directly across from it

parasitic: having to do with a living thing that lives in, on, or with another living thing and harms it

prey: an animal that is hunted by other animals for food

rare: not common

venom: a poison passed by one animal into another through a bite or a sting

FOR MORE INFORMATION

BOOKS

Bishop, Nic. *Spiders*. New York, NY: Scholastic, 2012.

Marsh, Laura. *Spiders*. Washington, DC: National Geographic, 2011.

Ray, Michelle. *A Huntsman Spider in My House*. New York, NY: Morgan James Kids, 2014.

WEBSITES

10 of the World's Largest Spiders
conservationinstitute.org/10-of-the-worlds-largest-spiders/
Visit this website to learn more about some of the largest spiders on Earth.

Fun Spider Facts for Kids
sciencekids.co.nz/sciencefacts/animals/spider.html
Learn amazing facts about spiders in general on this website.

Huntsman Spider
animalcorner.co.uk/animals/huntsman-spider/
Read more about the huntsman spider on this site.

INDEX

Asia 6

Australia 6, 10, 16

bite 18

caves 10

colonies 16

color 10

eggs 14, 20

fangs 12

fast 4, 8, 12, 13, 20

giant huntsman 4, 5, 6, 8, 10, 18, 20

hunt 4, 12, 16

Laos 6, 10, 18, 20

leg span 8

legs 8, 9, 10, 13

molting 14

mother huntsman 14, 15, 16

pest control 4, 18, 21

prey 4, 12, 13

silk 14

social huntsman 16

species 4, 6, 8, 10, 14, 16, 17, 20

spiderlings 14

United States 6

venom 12